FIRST-PERSON STORIES OF THE KOREAN WAR

BY TAMRA B. ORR

ROSEN PUBLISHING PRIMARY SOURCE LIBRARY

ROSEN PUBLISHING

Published in 2027 by The Rosen Publishing Group, Inc.
2544 Clinton Street, Buffalo, NY 14224

Designer: Deanna Lepovich
Editor: Nicole Horning

Cataloging-in-Publication Data

Names: Orr, Tamra B.
Title: First-person stories of the Korean War / Tamra B. Orr.
Description: Buffalo, NY : Rosen Publishing, 2027. | Series: The Rosen Publishing primary source library | Includes glossary and index.
Identifiers: ISBN 9781725343139 (pbk.) | ISBN 9781725343146 (library bound) | ISBN 9781725343153 (ebook)
Subjects: LCSH: Korean War, 1950-1953–Juvenile literature. | Korean War, 1950-1953–United States--Juvenile literature.
Classification: LCC DS918.O77 2027 | DDC 951.9042–dc23

Manufactured in the United States of America

CPSIA Compliance Information: Batch #CSRYA27. For further information, contact Rosen Publishing at 1-800-237-9932.

CONTENTS

FOREWORD

History is so much more than just a boring collection of names and dates. It is a collection of stories—sometimes tragic stories, sometimes heroic stories, sometimes romantic stories, sometimes scary stories. And they're all stories of real people who lived real lives.

Those stories can get lost in the shuffle of memorizing battles, studying maps, and listing important court cases or rulers. That's why primary sources are so valuable. They remind us that historical events happened to and because of real people. Reading diaries, looking at photographs, and seeing newspaper articles are just some ways to make history feel personal through primary sources.

Another way is through watching or listening to interviews with people who lived through major historical events. That's what you're invited to do in this book—and all the books that are part of the *Rosen Publishing Primary Source Library*. Each chapter includes quotes from an interview with a real person who experienced a major historical event in a deeply personal way. You can also scan the QR code included at the beginning of each chapter to watch a video interview with the person featured in that chapter.

Created in partnership with Generations Broadcasting, the *Rosen Publishing Primary Source Library* was created to remind readers that there is power in sharing our stories. First-person stories make history come alive. And when history comes alive, we're better able to learn from it—and avoid the mistakes of the past.

The events you're living through today will be part of the next generation's history lessons. As you read and watch the stories collected here, think about what you want your story to be.

Note: More interviews about the topics featured in this series, as well as many other historical events, can be accessed via a subscription to Rosen Publishing's GBC Stories Database: rosendigital.com/GBCStories/.

HOW TO WATCH THE INTERVIEWS FEATURED IN THIS BOOK

- Use your phone's camera, and hold it over the QR code.
- Click the link that appears.
- Watch the video that pops up. If you would like to read a transcript of the interview while you watch, you can click on that option in the video player.

INTRODUCTION

In the early 1950s, the world was still trying to find its footing after the destruction of World War II (1939-1945). Nations were rebuilding, alliances were shifting, and a new kind of global tension was beginning to take shape. At the center of this tension was the spread of Communism and the growing fear in the United States that entire regions of the world could fall under its influence. It was in this uncertain moment that a small peninsula in East Asia—Korea—became the focus of an international conflict that would last three brutal years.

In 1950, President Harry S. Truman made a decision that changed the course of history. Believing that if one country fell to Communism others would follow, he embraced what became known as the Domino Theory. If South Korea collapsed under North Korean forces, he feared that nearby nations, and eventually even the United States, could be threatened. When North Korea invaded the South across the 38th parallel on June 25, 1950, Truman responded quickly, sending American troops as part of a United Nations force. Although he called it a "police action" rather than a formal war, the fighting that followed was anything but limited.

For the soldiers who arrived in Korea, the fighting was immediate, confusing, and often overwhelming. Many had just returned from World War II or had only recently entered military life. Some were drafted, pulled unexpectedly from their everyday lives, and placed into a conflict on the other side of the world. Others volunteered, believing they were serving in a mission to defend democracy. All of them quickly discovered that Korea was a battlefield unlike any they had seen before. The terrain was harsh, the weather extreme, and the enemy forces determined and well-prepared.

Across the peninsula, the war moved rapidly and unpredictably. Cities like Seoul changed hands multiple times, and front lines shifted again and again. Soldiers fought in trenches filled with mud, freezing water, and constant danger. In the air, pilots engaged in high-speed battles. Beneath the sea, minesweeper crews risked their lives clearing paths for invasion forces. Meanwhile, civilians were

Thousands of lives were lost in the Korean War. Part of the Korean War Veterans Memorial in Washington, D.C., is shown here.

caught in the middle, struggling to survive in cities destroyed by repeated combat.

Despite the massive effort and sacrifice from multiple countries, the war gradually settled into a **stalemate**. Neither side could claim a clear victory. After years of fighting and millions of lives impacted, an armistice was signed in 1953, stopping the shooting but not officially ending the war. Korea remained divided, and the border at the 38th parallel became a permanent line between two very different nations.

This book explores the Korean War through the voices of those who experienced it and the events that shaped its outcome. From the first invasion to the final ceasefire, it tells the story of a conflict that was intense, global, and deeply human. Although it is often called "the Forgotten War," its impact continues to shape the world today.

CHAPTER ONE

A GAME OF DOMINOES

In June 1950, President Harry S. Truman made a decision that would pull the United States into a new kind of conflict on the Korean Peninsula. He believed that if Communism spread in Korea, it could spread across the world, putting other nations, including the United States, at risk. This idea, known as the Domino Theory, helped shape America's response in Korea, as troops were sent into what Truman called a "police action," not an official war (although it is most commonly known as the Korean War). While many Americans at home knew little about Korea, soldiers on the ground quickly faced danger, confusion, and fear. In an interview, Howard described patrols where soldiers were killed or captured without warning, showing just how deadly and unpredictable the war was from the very beginning.

THE UNITED STATES GETS INVOLVED

On November 30, 1950, President Truman held an important news conference to explain the ongoing conflict between Communist North Korea and democratic South Korea to the American people. American troops had been in Korea for nearly six months at that point, so Truman felt the need to explain the reasons Americans

Scan this QR code to watch Howard discuss some of the most frightening moments he experienced during his years of service in the Korean War.

Posters like this one from 1951 helped remind Americans why the Korean War was an important step in stopping Communism.

had been sent to the Korean Peninsula to fight. He believed that the United States, backed by the United Nations, had no choice but to get involved.

He told Americans that the United States would keep working not only to stop Communist aggression in Korea, but also increase the country's military strength and help other democratic nations also increase their military strength. Truman was concerned that if the United Nations yielded to Korea's threats of aggression, then no other nation would be safe, because this aggression would spread throughout Asia and Europe.

In 1950, Truman sent troops into what was being called a "police action." Thus began three years of a new type of national conflict.

A NEW THEORY

If you have ever set up a row of dominoes, you can understand why Truman's approach to the conflict in Korea was part of his "Domino Theory." He felt that if one country fell to Communism, it would be the first domino in a long row. When it toppled, the next one would

President Truman believed that if all of Korea fell to Communism, other countries like Vietnam, Laos, and Thailand would follow.

fall, and then the next one, until the entire line would be flat. The president felt that if South Korea became Communist, like North Korea, it would be that first domino. From there, Communism

The Korean War lasted for three years. Sixteen countries participated in the conflict.

THE FORGOTTEN WAR

The Korean War is often called "The Forgotten War" or "The Unknown War." But how could such a brutal conflict be forgotten by Americans? First, when President Truman announced that the United States was entering Korea, it was never with a formal declaration of war. It was referred to as a "police action." This reduced the feeling of it being a national emergency. Because there wasn't a sense of a national emergency or massive troop mobilizations, daily life for many Americans remained unaffected. There wasn't mandatory rationing like in World War II and there weren't shortages of materials. Life, for the most part, carried on as usual.

Additionally, televisions weren't widespread yet, and the war wasn't televised in the way that the Vietnam War would be later. The Korean War also wasn't covered in newspapers like the wars before or after it, which meant Americans were largely unaware of what was going on, resulting in a sense of indifference.

The war also occurred during a unique time in history when it was bookended by a few other crises. The Great Depression, which was a severe economic collapse that resulted in massive unemployment and bank failures, happened from 1929 to around 1939. Coming out of this national emergency, World War II started in 1939, but the United States didn't join the war until 1941 with the Japanese attack on Pearl Harbor in Hawai'i. The war had only recently ended in 1945, and Americans weren't prepared to go back to war so soon after World War II. They were tired of constant conflict and wanted to focus on postwar prosperity.

After the Korean War ended, the Vietnam War began, with the United States officially entering the conflict in the 1960s. The Vietnam War was

would ripple out in a chain reaction across the world until it inevitably reached the United States.

The Domino Theory focused on **containment**, or stopping the expansion of Communism. The first key to doing that, according to Truman, was to go to Korea with military force and stop North Korea's push. It wasn't an easy task. North Korea had the support of the Soviet Union and China, both extremely powerful nations. The United States, on the other hand, had the support of the newly formed United Nations, which included the United Kingdom, Canada, Australia, and Türkiye.

incredibly traumatic for Americans. The military draft was unpopular, and some people found out they were going into this brutal war on television through the draft lottery. Vietnam also involved very high casualties, an unclear mission, and new fighting grounds in thick jungles where soldiers couldn't see the enemy. Many soldiers returned home with mental health issues such as post-traumatic stress disorder.

The Korean War was in the middle of these long-lasting and traumatic events. As such, it's often forgotten or glossed over because other highly traumatizing wars dominated public memory.

A Korean War memorial refers to the war as a Forgotten War.

THE VIEW FROM HOME

As concerned as President Truman was about what was happening in Korea, the majority of Americans knew surprisingly little about the country or what was happening there. It was understandable. They had just survived

FAST FACT

THE KOREAN WAR WAS NOT TECHNICALLY KNOWN AS A WAR. INSTEAD, IT WAS A POLICE ACTION, OR A LIMITED MILITARY OPERATION.

Even though the Korean War is largely forgotten in the middle of much larger events, it was still a brutal conflict that many people fought and died in.

the horrors of the Great Depression, which ended with the start of World War II, which had just ended in 1945, and they were ready to return to a life without those kinds of international worries. Soldiers were home. The economy was improving. Televisions were entertaining families. The idea of another war and national crisis and all the money, casualties, and risk it involved was unthinkable.

FAST FACT

THE KOREAN WAR RESULTED IN A STALEMATE, WHICH MEANS NO ONE REALLY "WON" THE WAR. THERE WEREN'T HOMECOMING PARADES FOR U.S. SOLDIERS, WHICH MEANT THE END WASN'T REALLY CELEBRATED AND SOLDIERS DIDN'T TALK ABOUT THEIR EXPERIENCES, WHICH CONTRIBUTED TO THE WAR BEING "FORGOTTEN."

A DIVIDING LINE

Korea as a peninsula is divided in half by an invisible boundary known as the 38th parallel. North Korea was Communist-ruled and had the full

The 38th parallel was originally meant to be a temporary dividing line, but it became a permanent one once the nations on the two sides of it started following different regimes.

Countless soldiers from multiple countries led patrols around the clock in Korea. It was exhausting and frightening.

FAST FACT

NORTH KOREANS REFERRED TO THE KOREAN WAR AS THE "FATHERLAND LIBERATION WAR." IN 1953, A MUSEUM DEDICATED TO THE HISTORY OF THE WAR WAS BUILT IN PYONGYANG. EACH YEAR, THOUSANDS OF VISITORS COME BY TO REMEMBER WHAT HAPPENED MORE THAN 70 YEARS AGO.

support of the Soviet Union and China. South Korea was non-Communist and had the support of the United States and a number of other countries in the United Nations.

In the early morning hours of June 25, 1950, more than 100,000 troops from the Northern Korean People's Army crossed that dividing line of the 38th parallel and brutally invaded the South. This was the official first day of the Korean War. The first domino was falling.

While many Americans remained somewhat oblivious to what was happening in Korea, Truman began to send armed forces to the peninsular. And for the thousands of troops sent there, the fight was very real and very frightening.

Howard, a veteran, remembered being on patrol one day. His two scouts were in front of him. In an interview, he said, "The first one [scout] was killed, the second one was taken captive." That soldier was never recovered.

"On another **reconnaissance**," he added, "I went out to get as close as I could to the enemy positions. And my platoon sergeant ... he saw one of the Chinese soldiers come out of a bunker, and decided he was going to go out and capture him." However, it was an ambush, and his sergeant was killed.

The Korean War had begun, and at first, it was not going well for the South Koreans. Despite U.S. naval, air, and ground troops being sent into the fray, the fierceness of the North Koreans' attack took a heavy toll. Seoul, South Korea's capital city, was taken quickly, and American troops were forced back to Pusan (today known as Busan), a port in the South.

Was the conflict already over, and was democracy the loser?

HOW YOU SEE HISTORY

1. Why do you think that President Truman decided to call the Korean conflict a "police action" instead of a war?
2. Do you think that Truman's Domino Theory and his fear of Communism were warranted?
3. Why do you think so many Americans were unaware of what was happening in Korea?

CHAPTER TWO

ON THE GROUND AND IN THE AIR

It did not take long for the United States to respond to North Korea's invasion. Within two days, the United Nations authorized military assistance, and it was just in time. The city of Seoul, South Korea's capital, was captured the same day. South Koreans were absolutely overwhelmed by the attack. Their weaponry was no match for North Korea's tanks. This led to several frightening moments for U.S. troops fighting in Korea. In an interview, Glenn shared some of his scariest moments from his time serving during the war and what it was like to be a pilot in Korea.

ESTABLISHING A PERIMETER

Five days after that first invasion, thousands of American troops gathered at a Japanese air base, ready to jump into battle. The troops' immediate goal was to stop North Korea from reaching Pusan. When they arrived, however, they walked into chaos. The fighting was intense, and the regiments that managed to still be alive were retreating quickly. The Americans and their allies simply were no match for the fierceness of the North Koreans. Within a matter of days, hundreds of U.S. soldiers had been killed.

UN troops set up a **perimeter** around the city of Pusan,

Scan this QR code to watch Glenn share his memories of one of his scariest moments during the Korean War.

Pilots were incredibly important during the Korean War, as so many of the conflict's battles took place in the air.

along the Nakdong River. The UN troops gathered at the eastern bank and waited for the invaders to arrive. They did not have to wait long. Although skirmishes popped up, and lives were lost on both sides, by August, the line was still being held. Some veterans today believe that if the lines weren't held during this skirmish, there

FAST FACT

THE SOLDIERS FIGHTING FOR SOUTH KOREA CAME FROM ALL OVER THE WORLD. MANY WERE FROM GREAT BRITAIN, AUSTRALIA, AND CANADA. THERE WERE ALSO TROOPS FROM ETHIOPIA, COLOMBIA, THAILAND, AND THE PHILIPPINES.

Soldiers at the Pusan perimeter stood in trenches to fire at North Korean regiments trying to break through.

> **FAST FACT**
>
> THE FIRST BATTLE OF NAKDONG BULGE OCCURRED ON AUGUST 8, WHEN NORTH KOREA TRIED TO CROSS THE RIVER AND REACH PUSAN. THE BATTLE LASTED 10 DAYS AND KILLED 1,200 NORTH KOREANS AND 600 AMERICANS BEFORE THE NORTH KOREANS WERE PUSHED BACK.

wouldn't be a South Korea today. This is even more remarkable because the UN troops holding the lines were outnumbered by about 20 to 1. However, when thousands of troops from the Chinese People's Volunteers force arrived, the ground troops were suddenly overwhelmed. Fortunately, they were about to get some help from above.

A wounded soldier receives a blood transfusion at a medical aid station near the Nakdong River.

WELCOME TO MIG ALLEY

Much of the fighting during the Korean War took place in the air. On December 17, 1950, the Korean skies were the setting for history's first known aerial fight between swept-wing jet fighters. It took place between America's F-86 Sabres and the Soviets' MiG-15s. The area below the fighting was a wedge-shaped alley that stretched along the Yalu River. This area was so full of aerial conflicts that it became known as "MiG Alley."

The planes in these battles flew much faster and higher than planes of the past. The Sabres and MiGs, both single-seat and single-engine planes, looked a great deal alike, especially when soaring past at 700 miles (1,126 km) an hour. There were a few reports of pilots on each side accidentally shooting down other pilots on their side because the planes were hard to tell apart.

AN EXECUTIVE ORDER

More than two years before the Korean War began, President Harry S. Truman signed Executive Order 9981 in 1948. This order required "equality of treatment and opportunity" in the U.S. Armed Forces, regardless of race, religion, or national origin. It was a major step toward ending segregation in the military and opened the door for Black Americans to serve alongside white Americans in all branches of service.

When the Korean War began in 1950, many people expected the military to follow this new rule quickly. The United States needed large numbers of soldiers, and the war created pressure to use all available manpower. In some cases, this led to **desegregation** on the battlefield, especially in units that were formed during the war. However, change did not happen evenly or immediately.

Many military leaders and units still held on to long-standing traditions of segregation. As a result, Black service members often found that their experiences did not match what they had hoped for when they enlisted. Many believed they would serve in fully-integrated units, but instead continued to face separate assignments or limited opportunities in certain roles. Even so, Black service members served with courage and distinction throughout the conflict.

Over time, the demands of the Korean War helped speed up the process of integration. The military gradually became more unified, but it was a slow and uneven change. The experiences of Black Americans during the war highlighted both the promise of Executive Order 9981 and the challenges of making equality a reality.

All-Black units like the 24th Infantry Regiment were sent to the front lines in Korea.

This Sabre pilot climbs into the cockpit of this jet fighter on his way to another skirmish in MiG Alley.

LIFE AS A PILOT

Glenn was a pilot during the Korean War. In an interview, he said that one of his most frightening moments was flying a nighttime mission near Sinuiju, along the Yalu River. He could look down from his plane and see a MiG fighter base. The runways were often full of

FAST FACT

MORE THAN 30 AMERICAN SABRE PILOTS WHO WERE SHOT DOWN DURING THE KOREAN WAR HAVE STILL NEVER BEEN FOUND. THE SEARCH FOR THEIR REMAINS IS ONGOING.

Navigators and pilots prepare for a night mission over enemy territory.

FAST FACT

DURING THE KOREAN WAR, THE U.S. FORCES DROPPED 635,000 TONS (576,062 MT) OF BOMBS ON NORTH KOREA. THIS WAS SIGNIFICANTLY MORE THAN THE 503,000 TONS (456,313 MT) DROPPED DURING WORLD WAR II. ACCORDING TO HISTORIANS, THOSE BOMBS KILLED AS MUCH AS 20 PERCENT OF THE COUNTRY'S POPULATION.

MiGs just ready to take to the skies and shoot down American planes.

"We didn't fly [in] formation because you couldn't see anybody or any other airplane," he explained. "It was pitch black."

Pilots relied on SHORAN, or short range navigational systems that made use of radar technology. These were tools that guided aircraft in bad weather or total darkness. "You didn't have to see your target because it was all done electronically," said Glenn.

The pilots, he stated, would fly one behind the other, separated by 30 seconds and about 500 feet (152 m) in **altitude**. They had to avoid getting caught in the North Korean's search lights. "Our **salvation** was those MiGs were not equipped with radar," he added. "They couldn't find us."

"Going up to Sinuiju was a scary, scary thing," Glenn admitted. "We had one crew that aborted; they wouldn't even go. They saw so much antiaircraft fire that the pilot turned around, and he dumped his bomb someplace ... and flew back to Okinawa."

From the moment President Truman decided to send troops and support to help South Korea, he knew who he wanted in charge: General Douglas MacArthur. The president hand selected him, and the nation approved. He was a war hero due to his strong leadership during World War II. At first, the choice seemed like a wise one, as MacArthur succeeded in driving back North

Bombing bridges was common during the war. It helped disrupt troops so they could not travel from one region to the next.

General MacArthur attends a briefing session at Inchon in September 1950.

Korea from the 38th parallel. However, tensions were rising, and Truman was about to regret his decision.

HOW YOU SEE HISTORY

1. Why do you think some pilots refused to fly into MiG Alley and turned back?
2. How did faster, more powerful planes play a role in the Korean War? Why was radar an important tool?
3. Why do you think President Truman specifically wanted General MacArthur to lead the American troops in Korea?

CHAPTER THREE

DANGEROUS WORK

The Korean War quickly became a fight full of risks, surprises, and tough decisions. Early on, UN forces were pushed back toward the southern edge of Korea, and it seemed like they might lose the war. Then, General MacArthur made a bold and dangerous plan to strike back. Through it all, real people experienced the war up close. One of them was Art Mueller. In an interview, he described what it was like to be part of dangerous missions such as minesweeping the water to remove mines.

THE BATTLE OF INCHON

General MacArthur was concerned about what he was seeing in Korea. He knew that if North Korea could reach the city of Pusan, the war was likely lost. He asked President Truman for more troops, and his request was approved. But now MacArthur had to figure out where to land these new troops where they wouldn't be detected or captured. He decided on a sea approach from the Port of Inchon, on Korea's west coast. Other commanders disagreed with his choice.

Inchon was a challenging choice on several fronts. First, the only way to reach the harbor was through an extremely narrow passage nicknamed the Flying

Scan this QR code to watch Art discuss his time spent on a minesweeper.

In mid-September 1950, American forces landed at Inchon, which is sometimes spelled Incheon.

Fish Channel. A **tidal basin**, the water in this region rose and dropped more than 20 feet (6.1 m) daily as tides came in and went back out. Boats would have to line up to get through the channel and only reach shore at the precise moment of peak high tide.

The trip to Inchon on naval destroyers was further complicated by the weather. The troops had to get to Korea during a **typhoon**. The sea was incredibly rough, and the front ends of the boats often went underwater before popping back up to the surface.

There was also another hidden danger beneath the water. North Korean forces had filled the harbor with Soviet-supplied naval mines. Before any troops could land, those mines had to be cleared. Minesweepers were sent in ahead of the invasion to locate and remove them. Working close to shore and under the threat of enemy fire, these ships faced extreme danger. Some were damaged or sunk, and sailors lost their lives. But their work was essential.

In late September 1950, senior U.S. commanders, including General MacArthur, gathered for formal ceremonies to officially hand Seoul back to the Republic of Korea (South Korea).

Without clearing a path, the larger ships carrying troops couldn't safely reach the beach.

Troops stormed onto the shore of Inchon in September 1950. MacArthur's predictions had been right. The area was only lightly guarded, and a few hours after they landed on the shore, the U.S. troops had secured the harbor. Just a few days later, North Korea was forced to retreat, and the capital city of Seoul was taken back.

UNDER THE WATER

One of the most dangerous parts of the Korean War was the presence of naval mines under the water, like those that had been cleared before the Battle of Inchon. More than 400 square miles (1,036 sq km) of ocean hid thousands of underwater, Soviet-supplied, magnetic mines. These weapons were quite effective, damaging or sinking ships and causing about 70 percent of the U.S. Navy casualties in the war.

To fight this threat, the Navy relied on minesweepers. Using a set of wires called the "paravane," these ships cut the cables

This minesweeper ship was blown up by a magnetic mine during sweeping operations in October 1950.

that connected the mines to the ocean floor. When the mines floated to the surface, the ship's gunners exploded them. It was a very risky endeavor, and there were accidents where minesweepers actually collided with the very bombs they were trying to disable.

When Art enlisted as an ensign, he was told to report aboard a minesweeper. He had no idea what he was getting into. "I said, 'Where are we going?' And they said, 'It's top secret,'" he recalled. "We'll tell you when we get out to sea.'"

He first spent time in a ship in the Bikini Islands region where the military had tested atomic bombs. Next, he was transferred to a wooden ship. Since magnetic mines were triggered by the presence of steel, this type of ship was much safer. Art added, "It had three offices and 35 enlisted men. We would go out and get before the mines and [use] the paravanes to cut the cables."

Minesweepers like Art's ship played a vital role in operations such as the Battle of Inchon. By clearing obstacles hidden beneath the water, they made it possible for larger ships and thousands of soldiers to make it to the shore safely.

A MISTAKE IN JUDGEMENT

The UN's forces kept advancing, and, by mid-October, they had crossed North Korea's border and captured its capital of Pyongyang. While this was a huge victory, it also put these troops 40 miles (64 km) from the border of China. China had been warning President Truman repeatedly that if UN troops got too close to their border at the Yalu River, they would consider it

FAST FACT

ONE OF THE HEROES OF THE KOREAN WAR WAS SGT. RECKLESS. HE WAS A HORSE WHO HELPED TO CARRY SUPPLIES AND AMMUNITION TO REMOTE PLACES. HE ALSO HELPED MOVE INJURED MEN OFF OF THE BATTLEFIELD. A STATUE OF HIM STANDS IN THE NATIONAL MUSEUM OF THE MARINE CORPS.

This photograph shows Chinese forces swarming UN troops.

"FROZEN CHOSIN"

Winter in Korea can be brutal, with temperatures often dropping below freezing and staying there for weeks. In late November 1950, troops from both sides were gathered at Chosin **Reservoir** n northeastern North Korea. UN troops were outnumbered four to one by Chinese forces who had snuck in and surprise attacked.

Worst of all, the wind chill was -35 degrees Fahrenheit (-37 degrees Celsius). Weapons jammed in the cold, and even simple tasks became difficult. Bullet wounds sometimes froze shut, slowing bleeding but increasing the risk of infection. Sweat froze inside boots, causing painful frostbite that could lead to lost toes or feet. In some cases, frozen bodies were used as barriers for protection against enemy fire.

The battle lasted for 17 long, frigid days and became known as "Frozen Chosin." Despite being surrounded, UN forces fought their way south in a fighting retreat, breaking through enemy lines and evacuating thousands of troops and civilians.

Although UN forces were forced to retreat, many did not recognize it as a defeat, but a test of endurance and survival. In the end, approximately 4,400 UN troops were killed in the battle, with another 7,000 wounded or hurt by the cold. The Chinese had an estimated 37,500 soldiers killed, wounded, missing, or hurt by frostbite.

A battalion of Marines sets up a command post near the Chosin Reservoir in this image.

Shown here are MacArthur (left) and Truman (right) before the general was fired.

a declaration of war. Truman was worried, but General MacArthur reassured him that the Chinese were **bluffing**.

It was a catastrophic mistake in judgement. The Chinese meant precisely what they said.

The Joint Chiefs were scared and told MacArthur

FAST FACT

DURING THE BATTLE OF INCHON, SHIPS ONLY HAD A FEW HOURS TO LAND TROOPS BEFORE SHIFTING TIDES DROPPED THE WATER LEVEL AND LEFT BOATS STRANDED IN THE MUD.

to not bomb any areas within 5 miles (8 km) of China's border. MacArthur ignored these instructions. On October 25, Chinese troops unexpectedly crossed into North Korea and attacked the UN troops, taking them by surprise.

The results were devastating. UN forces were pushed back in a rapid retreat, losing much of the territory they had just gained. What had seemed like a near victory quickly turned into a longer and much more difficult war.

In April 1951, Truman fired MacArthur. He was worried that MacArthur was going against their policy and goals in Korea.

HOW YOU SEE HISTORY

1. Do you agree with Truman's ultimate decision to fire MacArthur?
2. What would you worry about most if you were a soldier on a minesweeper boat?
3. Why do you think some troops and leaders considered the retreat from Chosin Reservoir a success instead of a failure?

CHAPTER FOUR

FROM THE STREETS TO THE TRENCHES

The Korean War dragged on into a brutal, grinding conflict with no clear end in sight. In cities like Seoul, control shifted again and again, leaving civilians trapped in constant danger and destruction. On the front lines, soldiers lived in trenches where cold, mud, and nonstop fighting made survival a daily struggle. In an interview, John recalled how difficult the trenches were. As the fighting continued, new leaders, new strategies, and new sacrifices shaped the path toward a fragile end to the conflict.

THE ONGOING BATTLE FOR SEOUL

Controlling South Korea's capital city of Seoul was considered a top goal for the North Koreans. The fight to control it was a fierce one that went back and forth several times. Between June 1950 and March 1951, it was captured and then freed four times. The battles were often fought street by street, block by block, and countless South Koreans were killed for being "collaborators." Some were shot just for talking to the UN troops. Neighbors turned on neighbors, and family members reported their relatives.

Although North Korea captured Seoul early in the war, a few months later, UN troops

Scan this QR code to watch John describe what it was like to be in the trenches on Korea's front lines.

Marines fight in the street during the liberation of Seoul while Sherman tanks wait in the distance.

> **FAST FACT**
>
> MANY SOLDIERS WHO SERVED IN KOREA WERE DRAFTEES, MEANING THEY WERE RANDOMLY SELECTED THROUGH A MILITARY DRAFT RATHER THAN VOLUNTEERING.

liberated the city. Four months later, Chinese troops seized the city again, until, in an action known as "Operation Ripper," UN forces took Seoul back one more time.

While the South Koreans were grateful to have their city back, the price they paid was devastating. During each battle, they were forced to cope with everything from a severe lack of food to the threat of being shot on sight. Thousands of citizens lost their lives in these fights for control. Buildings and streets were destroyed, and because cars were also destroyed in the fights, people often had to walk everywhere. There was also no food for the citizens to eat, so children would follow soldiers around to try to get food.

DAYS IN THE TRENCHES

Other soldiers spent weeks, months, or even years fighting in trenches dug on the war's front line. It was a harsh, horrible

Soldiers in a trench were typically armed with machine guns and rifles. Some of the men wore packs full of spare ammunition.

WACS, WAFS, AND MORE

The Women's Armed Services Integration Act of 1948 permitted women to serve in active-duty roles in the Army, Navy, Marine Corps, and Air Force, which was a first in the country's history.

Women from across the nation stepped up. More than 120,000 volunteered to serve in the Army (WAC), the Air Force (WAF), the Navy Women's Reserve, and Women Marines.

While some women worked in offices and support roles, others were sent much closer to the front lines than they expected. About one-third of these women were trained in the health-care fields and served in Mobile Army Surgical Hospital (MASH) units, in evacuation units, or on hospital ships, where they treated soldiers as quickly as possible after battle.

Other women handled critical wartime jobs such as operating switchboards, relaying messages, tracking troop movements, and driving Jeeps for officers across dangerous terrain. Even in these roles, the risk was constant, and many found themselves unexpectedly close to combat zones.

Army Nurse Corps nurse Margaret Zane Fleming experienced this firsthand. On October 9, 1950, she found herself and others under attack. She and Chief Nurse Major Eunice Coleman hid in a nearby ditch during the battle. Once the battle ended, they immediately got out of the ditch and started treating the wounded. For the entire day, they worked on roadside, treating soldiers for shock and performing lifesaving operations In total, eight men died and several supply vehicles were lost in the battle.

way to live full of danger from many directions. Bullets flew by, and below freezing temperatures coupled with mud and flooding made these trenches bitterly cold. Rats attacked, and mosquitoes swarmed.

When John was sent to the front lines of the Korean War, he had just gotten married and then drafted. He had no idea what was waiting for him. "They sent us over to Korea and put us in the trenches," he said in an interview. "They never told us what

Nurses serving in the Korean War were often in charge of helping wounded soldiers communicate with their families back home.

a trench was or how to build it or how to defend it. Our mission was to hold that line."

John said that when you were shooting at the enemy, you were simply shooting at assigned areas: "The United States Army says, 'You shoot from here to here and the next guy shoots from there to there.'"

"I spent a whole year in the trenches," John explained. "You shot all day, and then, at night, you would sleep in the bunkers." Since the enemy would try to breach the line all night, John said

Soldiers learned to cook their rations in the trenches. They also spent hours shoveling mud and water out of the way. Sandbags were used to keep the flooding under control.

"It was a 24-hour day. If they get in the trenches, it becomes hand to hand [combat]. They never breached us."

John was in the trenches when a ceasefire order came through. "[At] sunrise, I was standing on about the highest hill around there to see what it was going to be like," he recalled. "There was a ceasefire at midnight. And when sunrise came, it was quiet and peaceful. They were over on their hill and we were on our hill ... They had no incident, no fire. That was it."

A NEW PRESIDENT

The ceasefire came about after years of turmoil. The Korean War had stretched on for three years and it was not making

Some dogs were so popular with the soldiers that they became ship mascots like Rusty.

much progress. More and more troops were being sent to the front lines. Almost 2 million people had served, and more than 36,000 Americans had lost their lives. People were suffering. The American people were unhappy, with almost half of them believing going to Korea had been a huge mistake.

FAST FACT

DURING THE WAR, THE ARMY USED 1,500 DOGS TO GUARD **DEPOTS**, GO ON PATROLS, CARRY MESSAGES, AND GUIDE MEDICS TO WOUNDED SOLDIERS. THE MOST COMMONLY USED BREED WAS GERMAN SHEPHERDS.

Armistice negotiations between North and South Korea, China, and the UN went on for months.

FAST FACT

THERE WERE 137 MEDALS OF HONOR GIVEN OUT DURING THE KOREAN WAR. THIS IS THE HIGHEST HONOR THAT CAN BE BESTOWED UPON A MEMBER OF THE U.S. MILITARY. IT IS TYPICALLY AWARDED BY THE THE PRESIDENT.

In 1952, the new U.S. president-elect, Dwight D. Eisenhower, knew that something needed to change and vowed to go to Korea himself.

Eisenhower thought that Truman's approach to the Korean situation was full of mistakes, and he vowed to end the stalemate. One way he tried to do that was by making some subtle threats that the United States was willing to bring in nuclear weapons to win the fight.

Negotiations between the UN, North Korean, South Korea, and China had been going on for months, and more than 135 meetings had been held without success. At last, by July 1953, all sides involved in the war were finally ready to sit down and end the conflict. This Armistice Agreement, signed on July 27, stated

President Eisenhower is shown here eating with soldiers in Korea during the war.

WHAT TRUCE MEANS . . .

To Your GI Son
To Our PWs
To Your Job
See Page 3

FAIR — Mostly fair tonight and Tuesday; a little cooler tonight, low 67; high Tuesday 85, low Tuesday night 68. Wednesday a little warmer. Sunrise 5:40, sunset 8:15.

CHICAGO DAILY NEWS

★ An Independent Newspaper ★

78TH YEAR—175 Tel. DEarborn 2-1111 MONDAY, JULY 27, 1953. ★ 30 PAGES 5¢

FINAL MARKETS RED STREAK

IT'S OVER, OVER THERE

He Signs for Us—
Lt. Gen. Harrison signs truce documents for the United Nations.

Guns Fire Till Last Minute

400 U.N. Planes Bomb Reds As Korea War Grinds to Halt

SEOUL, Korea—(AP)—The shooting stopped as if by a magic signal at 10 p.m. Monday, Korea time, in the 37-month-old Korean war.

(Since Korea is 14 hours ahead of Chicago in time reckonings, the cease-fire began at 8 a.m. Monday, Chicago time.)

For the war-sick men dug in at the front it was the end of 37 terrible months of bloodshed, frustration and death.

Shooting flared just before the fighting died. While ground fighting was all but nil in the final hours, mounting Communist artillery fire took its toll of Allied soldiers up to the last minute.

The last man to die may never be named. Nor, perhaps will the last hero.

He Signs for Reds—
North Korean Gen. Nam Il signs documents for Communists.

'Thank God,' Prays Wounded Soldier

Patients at Great Lakes Fall Silent After Bulletin

(Picture on Page 15)

BY JOHN JUSTIN SMITH

"Thank God, that's over."

It wasn't a real prayer, just an accidental one.

But it told the feelings of one wounded soldier as he listened to the news flash from Panmunjom Sunday night.

2 Full Pages of Pictures
Pages 15-30

The Bride Carried a Tray of Beer

S. Shore Line Asks Hike on Indiana Fares

GIs Rip Out Front-Line Bunkers

Here's Guide To Other Truce News

Beech Tells Of Signing

War Makes a Shabby Exit In Dull 10-Minute Ceremony

BY KEYES BEECH
Daily News Foreign Service

PANMUNJOM, Korea—The war nobody won is over.

It died as it lived on a note of shabby indecision. And to the very last it was bad theater.

Armistice Supervisors Meet Tonight

N.Y. Police Fire Accused Red

Race Results

1,349 Korea Veterans Return

Sen. Taft Delays Return to Capital

44th Death In Florida Crash

Pause to Pray

Baseball

THEY'RE NUMBERED

Woeful Willie's First Slip Leads to More

Today's Chuckle

You'll Find:

Stories about the ceasefire in Korea hit U.S. newspapers.

President Truman presents the Congressional Medal of Honor to three Korean War veterans in the White House's Oval Office.

that all hostilities would end, all military forces and equipment would be withdrawn, and prisoners of war would be released.

However, while the fighting had officially ended, the armistice was not a peace treaty. Instead, it was a mutually agreed upon ceasefire, and it was far from permanent.

HOW YOU SEE HISTORY

1. What do you think the hardest part of living in the trenches would be?
2. Why do you think control of Seoul changed hands so many times during the war? What does that tell you about the fighting there?
3. In what ways did soldiers have to rely on teamwork to survive trench conditions?

CHAPTER FIVE

FAR FROM PEACE

For three years, troops from around the world had sacrificed their lives and fierce battles had raged, but, by the end, almost nothing had actually changed in Korea. The North and South were still sharply divided at the 38th parallel. They still had opposing political regimes. And the people who had fought in this conflict were left to wonder what it had all been for. In another interview with Glenn, he described more of his experiences during the war.

GOING HOME—OR NOT?

One of the biggest complications to ending the Korean War was how to handle the thousands of prisoners of war (POWs) from each side. The 1949 Geneva Convention had clearly stated that prisoners of war should be released and **repatriated**. It seemed straightforward—simply send soldiers back to their home countries. But what happens if they don't want to go back? Thousands of Communist POWs, for example, did not necessarily want to return to North Korea or China. They were frightened of how they would be received there. Would they be punished for being captured? Finally, the concept of "voluntary repatriation" was offered. POWs only needed to be returned if they wanted to be.

Scan this QR code to watch Glenn describe the many missions he flew from Okinawa into Korea.

This map shows the line marking Korea's Demilitarized Zone.

This concept was not a popular one with many American politicians or the public. It was also upsetting to the Chinese and North Koreans. It created so much disagreement that the Korean War kept going for months longer while the question of what to do with prisoners of war continued. In the end, the Communists gave in to the idea of voluntary repatriation. While more than 82,000 Chinese and Korean POWs went home, another 50,000 chose to stay where they had been held. Many soldiers were psychologically damaged after their experiences and would struggle for years from the horrible abuse, fear, torture, and terror they endured as prisoners of war.

FAST FACT

MORE THAN 75 YEARS AFTER THE KOREAN DEMILITARIZED ZONE (DMZ) WAS FIRST ESTABLISHED, IT IS STILL THE SITE OF ARMED CLASHES AND BREACH ATTEMPTS ON A REGULAR BASIS. ACCORDING TO SOUTH KOREA, NORTH KOREA HAS VIOLATED THE RULES OF THE ARMISTICE HUNDREDS OF TIMES.

American prisoners of war were captured by Chinese troops.

FAST FACT

DURING THE KOREAN WAR, THERE WERE HUNDREDS OF THOUSANDS OF POWS. ACCORDING TO THE UNITED STATES DEPARTMENT OF DEFENSE, MORE THAN 170,000 UN TROOPS WERE CAPTURED, AND MORE THAN ONE-THIRD OF THEM DIED. ALMOST 66 PERCENT DIED FROM INFECTIOUS DISEASES LIKE TUBERCULOSIS AND **DYSENTERY**.

"THIS IS YOUR TARGET"

During the Korean War, Glenn flew a total of 27 combat missions over 6 months. Glenn flew out of Okinawa, Japan, his plane loaded with 4,500-pound (2,041 kg) bombs. "[We would] go up there, fly the mission, drop the bombs and then high tail it out of there as quick as we could to get back to Okinawa," he recalled.

Glenn's bomb wing would fly every three days. "Whether you flew or not depended on if they put your name in the roster to fly that particular mission," he explained. He was never part of the planning on where to fly. Instead, he and the other fliers were given an assignment. "We were just told, this is your target," he said. He would attend a briefing about the mission and then start the pre-flight check, getting the guns ready and ammunition loaded.

On a typical mission, Glenn admitted, "I would be shooting at nothing. It was

FAST FACT

THE US DEFENSE POW/MIA ACCOUNTING AGENCY BELIEVES THAT MORE THAN 80,000 SOLDIERS WHO FOUGHT IN THE KOREAN WAR ARE STILL UNACCOUNTED FOR OR MISSING. THE ORGANIZATION FIGHTS TO IDENTIFY ALL REMAINS DESPITE THE LACK OF COOPERATION FROM NORTH KOREA.

In 1998, officials from the United Nations Command Military Armistice Commission salute a casket containing the remains of a U.S. soldier killed during the Korean War and finally repatriated.

A Black American soldier is helped by several Australian troops after being set free by the Communists.

Pilots would return from combat missions and circle their carrier ships waiting for the next strike to be launched from the deck.

at night—you couldn't see anything." He thought of himself as more of a passenger on these flights except that "They [the enemy] were shooting at me from the ground with a lot of anti-aircraft fire."

Glenn added that the North Koreans would try to lock the planes into their searchlights because then they could send their MiG aircraft to shoot them down. "When you're in the searchlights, you're blinded," he described. "I never fired a round at anyone during all those 27 missions, but boy, I mean, let me tell you, they were shooting at me. It was a scary experience."

NORTH AND SOUTH KOREA TODAY

The goals that Presidents Truman and Eisenhower had for North and South Korea were not realized in the 1950s. Now, more than 70 years later, they have still not been achieved. South and North Korea are starkly different states.

Today, South Korea has a strong democracy and powerful economy, while North Korea remains under **authoritarian** rule with a strong focus on increasing its nuclear abilities. As of 2026, South Korea is led by President Lee Jae Myung. Myung's campaign emphasized strong relations with the United States, and while he hopes to achieve a better relationship with North Korea, he realizes that it would be quite difficult.

Modern South Korea is sparkling, beautiful, and thriving—something that Korean War veterans could never have imagined. Because South Korea focused on the education of its children when planning how to rebuild, the nation has become a powerhouse today.

Lee Jae Myung was elected president of South Korea in 2025. His term will last for five years.

As of 2026, North Korea's supreme leader is Kim Jong Un. Rather than a president, he is a dictator whose power was inherited rather than elected. Although Kim Jong Un has pledged to work toward denuclearization, these promises have not been kept. North Korea has continued to do missile tests and nuclear detonations, despite international outcry and sanctions.

During the Korean War, the Soviet Union supplied the North with military equipment and weaponry. Now, the situations have reversed, and North Korea is providing artillery shells, ballistic missiles, and drones to Russia to be used in its invasion of and ensuing conflict with Ukraine. South Korea, on the other hand, has given indirect support to Ukraine by providing financial, humanitarian, and non-lethal military aid to the country. Tensions between these two nations are still high, and this still affects other countries.

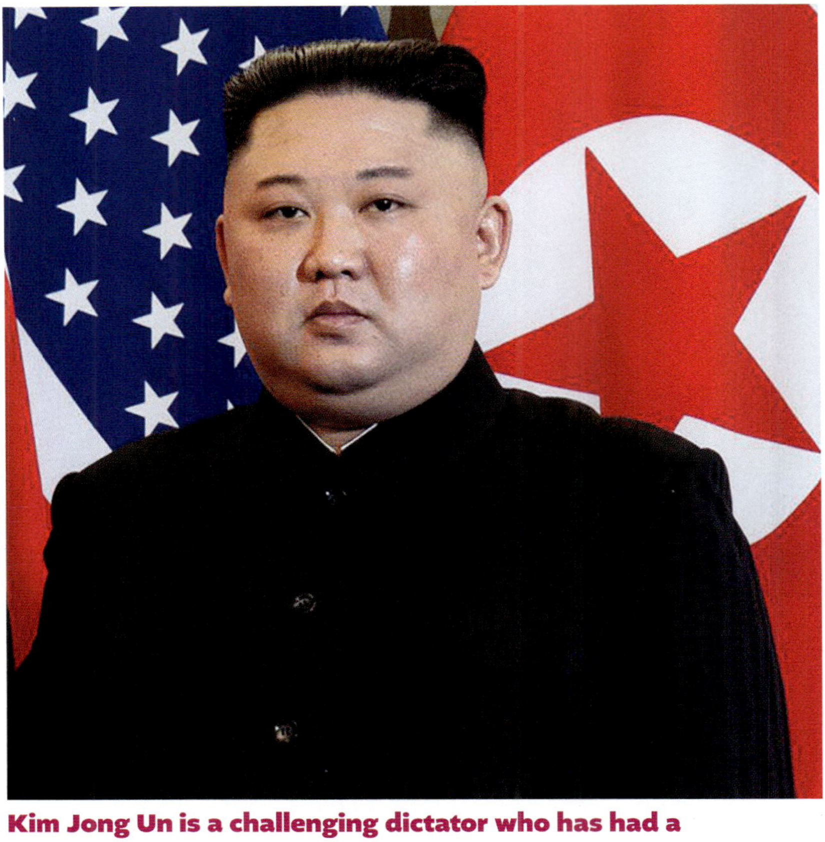

Kim Jong Un is a challenging dictator who has had a complicated history with the United States.

AN UNFINISHED PEACE

For three years, troops from around the world fought in brutal conditions and made enormous sacrifices, but by the end of the Korean War, almost nothing had truly changed. The Korean Peninsula remained divided at the 38th parallel, with North and South Korea still holding sharply opposing governments and beliefs.

In many ways, the war ended where it began—without a clear winner. A fragile armistice stopped the fighting, but it did not bring peace. Even today, the agreement remains only a ceasefire, and tensions between the two countries continue more than 70 years later. The Korean Demilitarized Zone (DMZ) is still heavily guarded and remains one of the most militarized borders in the world.

The human cost of the war was staggering. Hundreds of thousands of soldiers became prisoners of war, and many never made it home. Others returned with memories of dangerous missions where survival often came down to luck and skill.

Kim Jong Un shakes the hand of U.S. President Donald Trump in June 2018.

Today, South Korea has grown into a modern, thriving democracy, while North Korea remains isolated under authoritarian rule. The two nations that emerged from the war followed very different paths, shaped by the conflict that split them apart.

The Korean War is often called "the Forgotten War," but for those who fought in it, and those still affected by its outcome, it is anything but forgotten. It is a reminder that some wars do not end neatly, and some peace is still unfinished.

HOW YOU SEE HISTORY

1. What do you think the global community should do in response to North Korea's exploration of nuclear weapons?
2. The armistice stopped the fighting but did not create peace. What problems can happen when a war ends this way?
3. South Korea is worried about helping Ukraine too much during their battle with Russia. Why do you think getting too involved is frightening for them? What repercussions could their support have?

TIMELINE

A GAME OF DOMINOES: TIMELINE OF THE KOREAN WAR

1950: President Truman announces the United States' involvement in the Korean conflict.

1950: North Korea crosses the 38th parallel and captures Seoul.

ON THE GROUND AND IN THE AIR: TIMELINE OF THE KOREAN WAR

1948: President Truman issues Executive Order 9981.

1950: A perimeter is set up around the city of Pusan.

1950: President Truman names General Douglas MacArthur to lead the charge in Korea.

DANGEROUS WORK: TIMELINE OF THE KOREAN WAR

1950: American forces land in Inchon Harbor and recapture Seoul.

April 1951: President Truman fires General MacArthur.

November 1951: The battle at Chosin Reservoir occurs.

FROM THE STREETS TO THE TRENCHES: TIMELINE OF THE KOREAN WAR

1948: The Women's Armed Services Integration Act is passed.

1952: President Dwight D. Eisenhower is elected and vows to make changes in Korea.

1953: In July, the Armistice Agreement is signed, creating a ceasefire order.

FAR FROM PEACE: TIMELINE OF THE KOREAN WAR

1949: The Geneva Convention determines how to deal with prisoners of war.

1953: The Demilitarized Zone is created.

GLOSSARY

altitude: The height of anything above sea level.

authoritarian: Describing a political system in which individual freedom is held as completely subordinate to the power or authority of the state.

bluff: To mislead or fool.

containment: The act of restricting the territorial growth or influence of a hostile nation.

depot: A railroad station.

desegregate: To eliminate racial segregation or separation.

dysentery: An infectious disease marked by inflammation of the lower bowels, resulting in severe diarrhea.

perimeter: A line bounding or marking off an area.

reconnaissance: A search made for useful military information in the field.

repatriate: To send back home.

reservoir: A place where water is collected and stored.

salvation: The act of saving or protecting from harm.

stalemate: A situation in which no action can be taken or progress made.

tidal basin: An artificial body of water open to a river and subject to tidal action.

typhoon: A tropical cyclone.

FOR MORE INFORMATION

BOOKS

Downs, Kieran. *The Korean War*. Bloomington, MN: Torque, 2025.

Isserman, Maurice. *Korean War*. New York, NY: Chelsea House, 2010.

Rossiter, Brienna. *The Korean War*. Mendota Heights, MN: North Star Editions, 2024.

Sides, Hampton. *On Desperate Ground: The Marines at the Reservoir, the Korean War's Greatest Battle*. New York, NY: Doubleday, 2018.

Streissguth, Tom. *The Korean War*. North Mankato, MN: Child's World Stride, 2024.

WEBSITES

The Gilder Lehrman Institute of American History: Korean War

www.gilderlehrman.org/history-resources/essays/korean-war

This organization has essays, articles, images, photos, and much more on the Korean War.

The Harry S. Truman Presidential Library and Museum

www.trumanlibrary.gov/

This extensive website is dedicated to the presidency of Harry S. Truman, including almost 2,000 articles, photos, essays, and more on the specific role Truman played in the Korean War.

History.com's Korean War

www.history.com/search?q=korean+war

History.com has more than 30 pages of articles and photos on the topic of the Korean War, including links to television episodes and "This Day in History" features.

The Korean War Legacy Project

koreanwarlegacy.org/

This extensive site features multiple history articles and a very detailed memory bank of videos made by Korean War veterans.

PBS: The Korean War

opb.pbslearningmedia.org/resource/1d561db0-05bb-4838-8048-fc045db69c14/the-korean-war/

PBS offers maps, handouts, worksheets, videos and much more on many topics surrounding the Korean War.

INDEX

PHOTO CREDITS

Cover Everett Collection/Shutterstock.com; p. 7 ChicagoPhotographer/Shutterstock.com; pp. 9, 22, 23, 24, 51 courtesy of the National Archives; p. 10 Sarfaraz82/Shutterstock.com; p. 11 Korean War Montage 2/Wikimedia Commons; p. 13 DLeos/Shutterstock.com; p. 14 Jeff Morgan/Shutterstock.com; p. 15 Science History Images/Alamy Photos; p. 16 UtCon Collection/Alamy Photos; p. 19 Korean War aces/Wikimedia Commons; p. 20 27th Infantry Regiment soldiers at the Pusan Perimeter, September 4, 1950/Wikimedia Commons; p. 21 USMC Casualty Naktong River/Wikimedia Commons; pp. 25, 45 Alpha Stock/Alamy Photos; p. 26 FM Archive/Alamy Photos; p. 28 Battle of Inchon/Wikimedia Commons; p. 29 NH 96379 Liberation of Seoul, Korea, September 1950/Wikimedia Commons; p. 30 Eraza Collection/Alamy Photos; p. 31 Second Phase Campaign/Wikimedia Commons; pp. 32, 43 Everett Collection Inc/Alamy Photos; p. 33 President Truman and General MacArthur at Wake Island/Wikimedia Commons; p. 36 Seoul Battle- Korean War/Wikimedia Commons; p. 37 History and Art Collection/Alamy Photos; p. 39 NORMASH nurse Korea/Wikimedia Commons; p. 40 Australian soldier heats rations while another clears their trench/Wikimedia Commons; p. 41 80-G-429632 (32354988242)/Wikimedia Commons; p. 42 80-G-436371 Korean War Armistice Negotiations, Panmunjom, Korea/Wikimedia Commons; p. 44 John Frost Newspapers/Alamy Photos; p. 47 Peter Hermes Furian/Alamy Photos; p. 48 Smith Archive/Almay Photos; p. 49 Hum Images/Alamy Photos; p. 50 SuperStock/Alamy Photos; p. 52 Xinhua/Alamy Photos; p. 53 ZUMA Press, Inc./Alamy Photos; p. 54 Kim and Trump shaking hands at the red carpet during the DPRK–USA Singapore Summit/Wikimedia Commons.

ABOUT THE AUTHOR

TAMRA B. ORR is a full-time freelance author living in the Pacific Northwest. She has a degree in English and Secondary Education from Ball State University in Indiana. She has written hundreds of nonfiction/educational books for readers of all ages. Some of her titles include *Korean Americans* and *Korean Heritage*. She and her husband, four children, two cats, and one grandchild are all constantly reading and learning about the world (except for those lazy cats!). As a former homeschooler, Orr taught her children about important events in American history, such as the Korean War. (She admits those lessons were supplemented by watching every single episode of *M.A.S.H.*) Along with writing as a career, she is also a letter writer with pen friends from around the world. She designs her own cards and envelopes and almost always has either a pen or a book (sometimes both!) in her hand.